PAIR-IT BOOKS™
STECK-VAUGHN

Where Do BUGS Live?

Written by Jerald Halpern

STECK-VAUGHN®
C O M P A N Y

A Division of Harcourt Brace & Company

Bugs live in many places.

Where do bees live?

Most bees live in a hive.

Where do ants live?

Most ants live in the ground.

Where do butterflies live?

Most butterflies live in trees.